GOD HOLDS ME IN HIS ARMS

Raine's Journey

Raine Miller

ISBN 979-8-89043-351-0 (paperback)
ISBN 979-8-89130-329-4 (hardcover)
ISBN 979-8-89043-352-7 (digital)

Christian Faith Publishing
832 Park Avenue
Meadville, PA 16335
www.christianfaithpublishing.com

Printed in the United States of America

My Mission Statement

I am humble and grateful to say God has gifted me with the ability to teach, educate, counsel, encourage, mentor, evangelize, minister, and prophesy. My gifts have not all developed without pain, heartache, and difficulties.

Something I've learned through my life, and when I revisit my journals and reflect on the years, I've lived to see where I was one particular time and what was going on. I look back in amazement and say, "Wow, look at what I went through and how God allowed me to make it through." This is my journey, and I hope to encourage you in wherever you are within your journey. You, also, can make and will make it through. The key is to walk through the journey. Don't get stuck in one place, but allow yourself to walk all the way through to make complete to the end of your entire journey.

I've had some dark times and some challenges, and we all have unique occasions and circumstances we must endure. The key is to live through them, and allow the test to become a testimony.

The true strength is allowing ourselves to know that we are victorious, and we will overcome, regardless of the circumstances we are in currently in.

Often, I had to learn that the wilderness journey is inexplainable.

Contents

REJECTION

There are different variations and forms of rejection. The word *rejection* is defined as "not good enough, not included."

From the earliest onset of human interaction, you may experience the slightest form of rejection to include you're not being included in a reading circle by one toddler because another child wants to be selfish or your book being snatched away by another toddler or someone screaming, "It's mine! It's mine!"

As we grow older, various levels of rejection occur. One example is the last person to be chosen for the team in gym class or the last person to be chosen in a group.

Another level of rejection is when someone's parent or caregiver dies. They often feel left alone when their parent dies, especially if the person is a child.

Another level of rejection is when your feelings are not reciprocated from the person you are in a relationship with. For whatever reason, the person doesn't feel the same as you do.

ABUSE

There are various aspects and levels of abuse: child abuse, mental abuse, and sexual abuse.

There should never be an instance when someone has to experience either of these categories of abuse. Unfortunately, more often than not, many people experience volumes of abuse daily.

Child abuse usually occurs when a close member of the family or a friend of the family or trusted person in authority or a regular individual who is sexually disturbed and wants to have sex with minors, then grooms the child, meaning they become close to the child and gain the child's trust, and with that shows the child they can trust the predator or pedophile.

Repeated child abuse from the same offender usually occurs over an extended period of time because the child has become swayed to understand that no one will believe the child or listen to the child, and often threats for safety of the child and/or parent or caretaker of the child are put in place by the offender.

Mental abuse is usually combined with other abuses of sexual abuse and/or child abuse. A person is told negative things about themselves that may or may not be true, such as you have crooked teeth, your feet are too big, etc. Other things may be insinuating the character of that person, such as they are not intelligent or not educated. In sexual abuse, such as prostituting and sex slaves, incest, etc., the person is broken down to feel that the abuser is the only person that cares about them in an unhealthy manner or threatened harm if this abuse is told to someone. Some people may receive beatings and may be degraded.

I give God my real for real. I talk to God as if he is my absolute *best* friend and keep it real. There are times when I say, "God, now you know I'm working on this right here, so what are we doing? You and I, right now. How do I handle this? Do you think you might let me know quickly because if you leave me too long to think about this thing, you already know, I'm going to mess this thing up."

I always tell people, "Whenever God uses me to help you, minister to you, give to you, prophesy to you, etc., God has jokes because I am indeed a 'work in progress.'" I know God shakes his head on a daily basis, often throughout the day at me, and says, "My child, my child, what am I going to do with you?"

I say, "I know, God, bless you Father, and have mercy on me, and you KNOW I LOVE you, don't you, GOD?" as I shake my head.

I am working toward every day and moment of my life to hear my Father say, "Well done, my good and faithful servant," when I transition from this earth unto he and the heavens above. This is my ultimate goal in my life. God is my Daddy, Confidant, Provider, Counselor, Pastor, Teacher, etc. God understands when I am frustrated, hurt, don't feel well, scared, disappointed, curious, hungry, need guidance, question my decisions, don't want to be rejected, and don't want to be without money or wonder about something that needs to be paid. I've counted, thus far, five different valleys I had to walk through.

This is a book about my life, and hopefully my journey will make someone else know they, too, can walk through the valley of the shadow of death and come out of it victorious. This book will be profound with explanation.

The power of the Holy Spirit is evident in my life. I believe in purity, prayer. God will do what he promised to do. God has offered to release a supernatural power, and I receive it in the name of Jesus. The Holy Spirit is inside of me and ready to release the requirements. I will reach the maximum potential.

Domestic 3 Violence

Relationships

When you are in a relationship with someone, always remember there are relationships that add to your life and relationships that take away from your life. If a person isn't adding something good to your life, you need to subtract that negative and volatile attraction from you. You can continue to love and pray for that person, but in order for you to be the best you that you can be, you need to subtract volatile, abusive, negative behavior, and discouraging words and actions from your surroundings.

The death of a marriage

This is difficult because I have two daughters and virtually raised them on my own. I think highly of marriage, but I tell anyone who asks me, please accept the person who your mate says they are. Don't try to change that person. If he was hooked on substances, when you got with him, unless he wants to change on his own, he will remain hooked on substances and make you a substance abuser, if given the opportunity. Often, the substance abuser may get upset if you don't want to indulge in abusing substances with him. I wanted and knew that I deserved better for me and my kids. I deserved more than a husband and kids' father being in the streets, getting high, and spending his paycheck on drugs.

I am a survivor of domestic violence

Shouldn't love and respect go hand in hand? This is an excerpt from my diary.

If I'm the only person loving someone in this relationship, allowance of rejection occurs. Since I'm rejected, don't you think I should move to the next door? I want to be loved so badly. I think the only one who will and can love me the way I need to be loved and love me enough is Jesus. God put some people in my life, and the devil put some people in my life. They are with me when I am in the gutter and feel like I can't rise up. I refuse to not rise up. I'm better than that. I'm crying about the burden that he gave me with this man. I know I'm not supposed to reject the people God put in my life. Whatever I'm about to do with my life, I know I'm about to prosper. Heaven splits a portal in the time frame. I know you have more for me than this, God. I will walk into my destiny. I just need to be strong enough to endure this pain.

I endured another form of domestic violence: mental abuse. A man came into my life for a few years and was constantly angry at me for no apparent reason. When someone yells at you constantly, you feel scorned and abused.

Self-Worth

Coming into full circle of the treasure and gift I truly am.

The death of two best friends

My father, who was my absolute best friend, passed away when I was pregnant with my second child in 2000. It was one of the most painful things I ever had to endure. I felt as if a piece of my heart was torn from my chest. I will never be able to replace that piece. My daddy taught me about the street and how to always speak up for what I want and go get what I want. He treated me like a princess. When I was born, people told me my dad acted like an angel was born on earth. He handed out apples and oranges (he couldn't afford cigars) to random people at the hospital and smiled to the heavens above. I was his sidekick when I was little. Once I heard his keys at the door, I would run to jump in his arms and pull his shoes off. If he was leaving the house and not going to work, I would hurry and put my shoes and coat on and meet him at the door. Where he went, I went and loved to be my dad's shadow.

Another proud day of his life was when I was accepted to Howard University. He didn't like the area the college was located in. There were sites in the streets that young college students in the well-known District of Columbia shouldn't necessarily be privy to while walking back and forth to get to campus, but he accepted the fact that his baby wanted to attend college in the District of Columbia. I can honestly say, I didn't choose a man of my dad's caliber to love me. I chose a subpar man who didn't treat me like a princess.

My mother, who was my other best friend, passed away in 2011. I can only describe the death of my mother as another piece of my heart that was ripped away with her death. The pain is indescribable and, at times, seems unbearable. She taught me the Bible and about God, and it is through her and how she lived her life like an angel on earth that I can honestly say I am closer to God and humble and grateful to be a servant of God. I know God is real, divine, caring, loving, merciful, in the blessing business, faithful, etc. When I look at people God made to live on this earth, I know that my mom was one of those people. I was honored to be her daughter. She was my rock and my prayer warrior and my angel, and now she is my angel in heaven. Psalm 91:2 is my anthem for this heartache and hurt. Psalm 91:2 and Psalm 23 were some of her favorite Psalms.

The death of relationships of friends that I thought would always be with me

I had to learn to let go of the friends I had to buy their friendship in order for them to stay my friend. There was one point in life when God allowed me, didn't necessarily tell me, but I did purchase a car for a man and his family. I used to buy groceries and fill kitchen cabinets full of food for another family, a young lady with a family of six children. I paid $1,500 rent over six times in seven years for the man who said he was in need. I bought the car for him and his family and performed numerous deeds for people who I considered friends, but once I lost my job and didn't have income, none of these people asked if my children and I were okay. None of these people helped a single parent raise her two kids. None of these people texted me on any given day to include my lowest depressed days to simply say, "I'm thinking about you and love you." Not one person who I helped in the past gave a damn if me and my kids were surviving, hungry, naked, sleeping on the street, etc. I decided to look to God and Psalm 121 as my verse for faith and lean on. This Psalm became my anthem to heal this wound.

An excerpt from my diary: "When I press on toward Christ in my own life, I will make progress, and I ask God constantly to help me measure my maturity. When you add your individual days of your life, it makes a whole because getting caught up in the pressures of each day makes me need to look at my spiritual life. I realized I can't listen to my feelings more than I act. I can't let my feelings rule my life. Because I feel guilty or less than doesn't mean I am guilty or less than. God simply used me to advance others."

I also learned that God holds certain things back from me in order to bless me. God has to process me first, then God can give it to me. I had anger and identity crisis as to what God wanted me to do. "Am I getting married? Do I have a ministry within me? What gifts do you want me to use?" God has blessed me with more than one gift. I'm so humble and grateful, and I make sure I use my gifts when God allows me to (Romans 12:6).

The death of a relationship between a child and I

I carried her in my stomach for nine months, nurtured for years, encouraged, loved so very much, and provided for as best as I could. When she didn't need me to be a part of her life anymore, she allowed herself to get to a point that her disrespect for me, and I think she is embarrassed because I've struggled so badly and been without work, and we lost things along the way before God provided me with another opportunity to work, that she told me one day, she wished her dad had killed me the day she saw him put his hands on me. She told me she would never respect me and hated me. Yes, I am brave enough to tell you this story. When you read this, I know it will help someone else that is going through this or something similar. I chose after this to continue to love my child but at a different level. I could not allow someone I carried in my stomach, fed, clothed, nursed in sickness, etc. to feel disrespect would be warranted.

One thing is for sure, God will display the will of God in your life if you walk according to his plan(s) he has for you. Everything will never be perfect. You will have difficulties, discouragements, and questions, but when you focus on the fact that God is in control of your journey and lay your life down in God's hands, you will be okay. Always encourage yourself and maintain the will of God.

Speak life into your life. I refuse to speak negatively over my circumstances, even when the obvious is seen. I declare God is good and God is good all the time. I speak to the mountain and declare God is real and speak blessings into my life. Please speak blessings into your life. Please speak prosperity into your life.

Many people fail because they never have the courage to be who they are. Whatever God has told me to do, I need to do and will do. Whatever God has put in my heart, I need to go for it, and I will go for it (Joshua 1:7).

FINANCIAL 5 STABILITY

The death of financial stability

I lost my job for four years straight, and no one would hire me for a job. I won't say I couldn't find a job because that is not how my life is. I found many jobs and applied for over eight hundred jobs in a four-year period and interviewed for well over fifty during the four-year span. My children and I suffered for a four-year period, but through suffering, I knew God even more. I think it's fair to say, my children saw through my perseverance and determination to obtain another job, and they saw strength within me that a normal human being couldn't have. I told them each day and others who said I was their modern-day Job from the Bible or their "*shero*" that God is teaching me to only depend on God's goodness, mercy, grace, provisions, and blessings. The manager at McDonald's told me

I deserved a position where my résumé had outlined my numerous years of work experience, and he was sure I would be hired soon.

Three more years went by after that interview, with no job. I wanted to beg him to hire me for the $9.50 an hour job. I often wondered if I only threaten someone with a gun to their head who interviewed me and said, "Listen, I will show up here on Monday, work with you, and you will pay me on Friday." That was a joke, but I used to wonder, *What else do you want? I pretty much begged you to hire me and said, "Please pay me this $9.50, my kids and I are hungry. I need to pay for the roof over my head. I need an income. Forget about my résumé. Just give me the chance to work with you."* I looked to Psalm 27 as my anthem for this heartache and hurt.

LIFE

Speak a healthy and loving life over your life on a daily basis. The daily flow of life can be challenging and sometimes overwhelming. It's how you choose to cope with your daily challenges and responsibilities is how you will conquer the difficult situations that occur. "Life happens." Yes, it does. You make sure you live life. It takes practice. Everything with practice becomes perfect. You practice it to perfection. Either it's a habit or routine, it doesn't matter. It takes approximately forty days to form a habit. Form positive habits. Push pass the temptation to take on negative attitudes, situations, people, etc. You have a choice who you build a friendship with. Don't try to fix anyone. That's not your job. Most relationships I've had with men, I thought I needed to help them. I'm not God. I had to come to the harsh reality that I can't fix anyone, and they don't need me to fix them. Get over it.

Fix myself and make sure I don't bring any trash into my life. If you become a crutch for someone, trust me when I tell you, you will become their hospital. They will only seek you out when they are injured and need a Band-Aid.

Nothing is wrong with praying for someone. Pray God's will be done for them. It's exceedingly difficult to keep going on day-to-day when you are in a depressed state or depression is your condition. When I say condition, I am referring to someone who lives their life every day in a depressed state of mind. They never find happiness in anything. They never see the possibility of hope in any matter of concern. They have a negative outlook and feel defeated in every aspect. Share this and pray for those in deep depression. Get rid of barriers and hindrances. I know God didn't want you or me to be depressed.

7 HEALTH

Being healthy is worth more than any amount of money you could ever have. If your health is diminished or fails, time doesn't slow down for anyone. You have to make sure your mindset, eating habits, friendships, and daily activities involve healthiness. I'm not by any means judging anyone for anything you do. I am simply saying, firsthand, when you eat a lot of junk, your body will feel sluggish and like a wasteland. No one wants a wasteland as their heart, kidneys, liver, stomach, pancreas, esophagus, colon, uterus, lungs, etc.

I know it's hard to drop unhealthy habits. Unfortunately, so often it takes a near-death experience like a heart attack, shortness of breath, routine doctor visit, and a callback saying there is an irregularity in your lab work or we need to test you for this or see what this mass is, etc. Let's not get to the point where we need the doctor to tell us that you can do better. For example, parking your car in a far parking space and walking that extra distance. Some people walk stairs or take daily walks around the block or park. Whatever you are comfortable with is what you should practice.

Hebrews 10:33 says, "Sometimes I have been publicly exposed to insult and persecution and other times I've stood by those who were mistreated. It's my decision to not stand in an affliction but go through the journey."

I speak and believe this daily: "Affliction is broken over my life. I refuse for affliction to come into my way. The affliction is lifting from my life. I am not a prisoner of affliction."

Mental 8 Stability

When I think positive thoughts, positive results will occur. I personally feel that peace has to be deeply embedded in me spiritually, so deeply that my mind can't conceive negativity. My relationship with God is not material or cognitive or intellectual. It's spiritual. God is molding me uniquely mentally. I don't understand what God is doing, but God is strengthening me for a circumstance that my mind doesn't even know is on the way.

A healthy mental state is when you decide to let the fear subside. I don't have to feel fear to be afraid. I know God is not the author of fear. Courage is when I take the action I know God wants me to take while I feel fear, and I will not fear. It means that I can feel the fear, do whatever I believe that I am supposed to do while I feel afraid, but I won't let the feeling of fear keep me trapped or bound. I have faith that better things will happen for me.

A Word from the Author

I am grateful for the opportunity to share my journey through some of my valleys with you in a deep desire to help you along your journey. If I can make it, you can also make it. Stay encouraged throughout bad days, stay strong, stay focused, and please remember, you are resilient. I am a direct result of believing and trusting in God's goodness, and I know God is not finished with me yet. When you feel weak, pray. Pray often. This will allow the tranquility of peace to renew your mind. I hope my journey has helped you. I love you, and God loves you also.

About the Author

 Raine Miller lives to promote goodness and positivity within herself and others. After four decades of many paths within her roads through this journey of heartache and betrayal, she will use her hurt, pain, suffering, etc. to help you understand you also can make it through this pain. God loves each of us. Let God show the love God has for you.